Pulp Cutters' Nativity

Other Works by David Budbill

Poetry
> From Down to the Village
> The Chain Saw Dance
> Barking Dog

Plays
> Knucklehead Rides Again
> Mannequins' Demise

Short Stories
> Snowshoe Trek to Otter River

Novel
> Bones on Black Spruce Mountain

Children's Book
> Christmas Tree Farm

Pulp Cutters' Nativity
A Christmas Poem in Two Acts

being
a contemporary adaptation
of the medieval English
miracle play
The Second Shepherds' Play

by David Budbill

Countryman Press
Woodstock, Vermont

© 1981 by David Budbill

© 1981 drawings by Lois Eby

CAUTION: Professionals and amateurs are hereby warned that *Pulp Cutters' Nativity*, being fully protected under the copyright laws of the United States of America and the Universal Copyright Convention, is subject to a royalty. All rights, including professional, amateur, motion picture, television, recitation, public reading, radio broadcasting, and the rights of translation into foreign languages, are strictly reserved. All inquiries regarding this play should be addressed to the author in care of Countryman Press, Woodstock, Vermont 05091.

Library of Congress Cataloging in Publication Data

Budbill, David.
    Pulp cutters' nativity.

    1. Jesus Christ—Drama. 2. Christmas plays.
I. Second shepards' play. II. Title.
PS3552.U346P8   812'.54   81-12506
ISBN 0-914378-79-1   AACR2
ISBN 0-914378-80-5 (pbk)

for my Father

Stick up for the little guy, Bud.
R.J. Budbill

Acknowledgments

To Ned Hitchcock and his students at Goddard College, Plainfield, Vermont, for the Haybarn Theatre production of this play in November of 1979 . . .

To Rob Lanchester and the actors at McCarter Theatre, Princeton, New Jersey, for the staged reading of this play as part of the Playwrights-at-McCarter series in November of 1980 . . .

To David Lampe, of the State University College at Buffalo, whose involvement with and expertise regarding medieval theatre was invaluable in helping recast the Afterword . . .

To Reathel Bean, actor/friend, whose enthusiasm for this play made possible the McCarter Theatre production . . .

To all these people I want to express my gratitude and thanks.

Characters

(in order of appearance)

The Flute Player:
The flute player wears an old pair of rubber-bottom, leather-top boots — sorels. Her wool pants are torn and dirty as are her three wool shirts and the greasy insulated vest she wears over them. Her leather mittens are old and holey. An enormous head of unkempt, frizzy hair gangles from under her dirty toque. In short, the flute player is filthy, tattered, more ratty than anyone you have ever seen. She is a parody of rags, a north woods reincarnation of Harpo Marx.

Antoine:
A pulp cutter and a French Canadian in his early fifties. Antoine wears a quilted red, fiber-fill jacket he bought at the discount store. The guts dangle here and there from tears. It is stained and dirty. His heavy, green woolen pants have many patches skillfully applied. His rubber boots have holes and patches too. He wears a toque and leather mittens. Although his clothes are old and worn, he wears them well and has about him an air of neatness.

Doug:
A pulp cutter, in his middle thirties. Doug wears red and black checked, wool hunting pants, old ones — torn and dirty. The pants are tucked inside his ten inch, insulated, leather boots. Once, a long time ago, these were good boots and quite expensive. Doug wears a ragged, blanket-lined denim coat, and a hard hat liner on his head, the flaps pulled down, the strap snapped beneath his chin. Like Antoine, he has leather mittens.

Donny:
A pulp cutter, in his early twenties. Donny is tall and thin, blond, good looking, quiet and shy. He has green wool pants too and sorel boots. Instead of a jacket, Donny wears many shirts, in the manner of the flute player, that way even though all the shirts are somewhat holey, the holes don't match and therefore he has cover. Donny also has a toque and leather mittens. Although Donny's clothes are dirty, he's not as ragged as the others. He's new.

Arnie:
The thief and Joseph, forty. Arnie wears a filthy, ragged, black and green Johnson Woolen Mills jacket that's too big for him, and dungarees, new ones, still blue, and a gray woolen cap with earflaps up. His rubber boots are like Antoine's — only cheaper and more worn. He wears green cotton work gloves. Arnie shaves once a week on Saturday nights; this is Thursday.

Gil:
Arnie's wife and Mary, forty. Gil is tall, big boned, fat, loud and ugly. She wears a faded house dress, garish slippers, no socks or stockings. Her hair is short and unattended.

The Angel:
A young woman, lovely, well endowed. She wears a white waitress's uniform — a tight fitting blouse, a mini skirt, a frilly apron. She is the flute player transformed.

The Baby Jesus:
A doll.

Setting

Time:
Christmas time, one morning, just after dawn.
The sun is not yet up. It will rise
during Antoine's opening monologue.
The temperature is twenty degrees below zero.

Place:
Somewhere in northern New England.
The landing of a pulp wood operation. Piles of pulp
stacked here and there. Foreground: softwood logs,
full length, waiting to be bucked. An old, dilapidated
crawler tractor with a winch. Some fifty-five gallon drums
of gas and oil and smaller cans of gas and oil
for chainsaws. Pulp hooks, peavies and somewhere
a pile of empty beer cans, plastic bags
and other litter. Evidence of a campfire.
About a foot of snow. Here at the landing
the snow is mixed with mud, wood chips, bark
and dirty oil.

Pulp Cutters' Nativity

Prologue

In the half-light of dawn the flute player enters from the woods
and clomps to the center of the landing where she removes
her snowshoes and sticks them in the snow.
She inspects the equipment, the crawler,
etc. Then she notices the audience, does a double take,
moves down center, bows formally to them then curtsies.
She takes off her mittens and lays them
ceremoniously at her feet and extracts from inside her shirts
a soprano recorder on which she begins to play
We Three Kings of Orient Are.

The first time through the verse and chorus she plays
sweetly, tenderly. The second time through she begins
to snycopate the beat, alter the phrasing until
when she reaches the chorus for the second time
she is playing a joyous, whimsical jazz improvisation
of the melody. This continues for the duration of the
improvisation, however long it may be, then she returns
to the verse and begins slowly to revert to the delicacy
with which she began, which she does fully by the time
she reaches the chorus.

The flute player puts the recorder back inside her shirts,
bows again, curtsies again, puts on
her mittens — ceremoniously, picks up her snowshoes
and exits.

A pause, then . . .

ACT I

Antoine enters mumbling to himself.
He paces back and forth in front of the uncut logs,
slapping and hugging himself, banging his mittened
*   hands together,*
stomping his feet, exhaling like a work horse.

   Antoine:
Shidacat'sass! Freeze like a turd!
Bull an' jam here outin da snow
so cold touch ho' fall right out!

An' dese pants ain't wuth tew cents,
so ain't this discount jacket
an' these boots got cracks
from las' year. May as well be out here
dressed in mah bikini.
Freeze like a turd.

   to audience

Ah'm gettin' old. Ah can't take this shit
much longer. And then what ah do?
Live on dat friggin' Social 'curity?
'baout enauf buy a can a peacesoup once a month.
Ah work longer 'an da sun, da lazy basserd.
Ah be here 'fore he get oudda bed,
be here still when he gone hum.

An' fer what! Make friggin' 50, 80 dollar
a week, tear my gut out fer dat.
An' ah work forenoon Saturday
just for da government. Da snooty basserds,
take it all! Every friggin' penny!
Ah be better off collect da checks,

stay ta hum, sit by da stof
rock away da winner
like ah use' ta be.

It ain't no use. Ah never get ahead.
Da friggin' politicians tax da pants
right off mah wimens. Ah got nathin!
Ah never had nathin. My Poppa,
he never had nathin. Ah tell dat
to them Washin'tonians they say,
"That's okay. We take it!"
An' fer what? So they can waltz araound
down there and fuck dere sec'ertaries
'steada eatin' lunch! Fuck me!
It be a goddamn miracle sent down by God
da likes a me ever make a decent livin'.

Thieves, all of 'em. Bad acters, ever' one.
Fuckin' no counts, two cylinders.
Robbers what they be, 'ceptin' you can't tell it
'cause they wear a suit!

Now you take some poor basserd
up in dis forsaken place, let 'im steal
a chainsaw or a caow, see what happen!
Lock 'im up right naow!
Mister man, I mean right naow!
An' why they do that?
Cause he be a thief? Poof!
They lock him up 'cause he be stupid!
He be too daum ta wear a suit!

Okay. You take me. Say I write my Senator,
say, "Ah'm sorry, sir, but ah be too poor
ta pay da taxes so don't you bother
send a bill." Ah wake up nex' mornin'
in da clinker wi' da chicken thief,
an' mah wimens and da babies be alone.

An' da ones we got right here ta hum,
da ones down to state capitol
is even worse. Come time dey be elected
they caum 'raound shake mah han' say,
"Ah work fer you, ah be yer sla'f
daown to da capitol." Talk 'bout straight
as serpent did ta Eef. Then dey get elected
an' you see how their noses get a funny color
from bein' up da touch ho' a da millionaires
too long. You see 'em on da street say,
"Ho! ah be Antoine, 'member me?"
Dey push you round like you be stick a pulp.

What's dah use? It never be no diff'ernt
'an it be right now. It never was. It never be.
No use. Piss and moan is all ah ever do,
'cause it's all dere is for da likes a me.
At least it make me feel a little better some.
Preach at dis pile a wood; keep me
from breakin' windows like da niggers and da kids.
Now all they got ta do is get them odders
talkin' just like me; get dem niggers off da streets,
then dey got not trouble 'tall.
Got us all
just exactly where they wan' us.

    turns away from audience, paces, then, to himself

50, 80 dollar a week
an' a hernia ever' day. Shit.
Basserds. Crooks. Two cylinders.
No use.

    paces

Bull and jam. Freeze like a turd.

    Doug enters

Antoine:
By Jesus, where ya been? Iss
da middle a da afternoon.

Doug:
Couldn't drag myself outta bed.
My back is killin' me. That goddamn crawler
is about to do me in. Pinched a nerve or somethin'.
Hurts like hell.
And this weather don't help neither.

I always thought that Hiram was a crazy stupid fool,
but maybe he ain't; maybe he knows what he's talkin' 'bout.
He was sayin' t'other day he thinks this ugly weather's cause
of all that walkin' on the moon or 'cause
them bombs punch holes into the sky. Hell, you know it's
somethin' what ain't natural.

Two years ago it was so dry I got no hay a'tall. Come this
    summer
got hay standin' to my waist but it's so wet
ya couldn't drive a tractor down the road.
Ain't natural.

Spring comes too late, fall comes too early,
but it's worse than it ever used to be.
And the birds ain't actin' right.

This September and October wet as May and June,
and now, Christmas Eve and 20 below;
this is February weather! Ain't natural.

Too goddamn cold too soon!
This morning when I stepped outside and went to blink
my eyeball froze right open and my feet froze to my shoes.
It don't make it easy.

Antoine:
Naow!

Doug:
Well, there's only one thing worse than all this crazy weather
and that's what's called the holy state of matrimony.
Holy, hell! It's like livin' with the devil.

You go out and get yourself a hen, she clucks around
for about a year or two, then she gets broody
and she begins to cackle; you get too close that hen'll
peck ya. She'll sit around all day, watch them soaps
and all the time be eatin' up your money.

Christ, if I'da known I'da never done it.
It's a terrible price to pay for rollin' 'round the bed.
Jesus! how I wish I'd been smart like Donny. Stay away
from church and all that marryin' stuff. I wish I'd been
like him. Stop in at night, see his little lady, dip in
and go. That kid is free! Ain't locked
inside a henhouse every night.

Hell, it's too late for me. I'm a domesticated cock,
and what's worse there's only one hen in my flock.
Sometimes I think that Albert's got the right idea.
Have five of 'em so you can be a decent rooster.
But every time I think that way I remember what he's got.
I'm locked up with only one, that poor bastard,
he's had five. No wonder he can't talk. Probably
they cut his tongue out, cut out t'other one too.
Some cock he is, can't crow or fuck;
no wonder he's so ugly.

By Jesus, I'm a slave for life
but I can see it could be worse.

    to audience

Listen boys out there, stay the fuck away from church.
Don't be like me and spend your life
wishin' you were somewhere else and cryin'

to yourself 'bout how you didn't know how it would be.
Take it from me, she can catch you in a minute,
then she'll be done, but you'll have that chain
around your chicken leg for all your days.

You catch one and you think you've got
a sweet young thing, soft as a puffball on a tree.
You get her home and mister you have got a witch,
she'll change into a bully spruce so rough
it hurts to look. And ugly! Christ!
you just don't know. She'll drink your booze
and eat your food, get fatter than a sow.
She'll piss and moan and scream at you.
She'll belch and fart and lock you out.

Don't do it boys! Don't you get caught.
By Jesus Christ, I wish to hell
I'd run until I'd lost her.

   Antoine:
Shitagoddamn! Soun' like you climb onto
Canadian thistle. A burr in yer ass this mornin'.
Ah always taught yer little wimens
be gentle as a doe. What happen ta you?

   Doug:
Ah, things ain't workin' out just right.

   Antoine:
Wall, ah be here ta listen
if yew wanna talk.

   Doug:
It's nathin'.
It'll all blow over, maybe.

Where the hell is Donny?
Damn near seven o'clock.
If he'd work that dink a little less
and run the chainsaw more
maybe we'd get somethin' done.

> *Antoine:*

Caum on now, Doug.
You take it easy on dat boy.
He be good worker an' yew know he be.
You wass a kid once too.

Caum on, ah make a fire, warm are han's
before we go ta werk.

> *Antoine builds a fire and as he does, Donny enters carrying two chainsaws.*

> *Donny: (shyly)*

Sorry I'm late. Hard to get up.
Christ, it's cold! That bed is better than this place.

> *Doug:*

Sure it is, 'cause she kept sayin'
"Don't go! Don't go! I want some more."
You sharpen those saws?

> *Donny:*

I sharpened 'em.

> *Doug:*

Where's yours?

Donny:
Down to the woods.
It didn't need it.
Only needed touchin' up.

Doug:
That's no surprise.
It don't dull if it don't cut!

Donny:
What's eatin' you!

Antoine:
He have bad night. His back iss sore.

Doug:
That ain't it! We're losin' money
with this equipment standin' here.
We got to get goin'!
And this kid here better make up his mind
if he's gonna cut pulp or fuck around.
He's been late all week!
I ain't out here for my health, ya know.

Donny:
Lemme alone!
I told you I was sorry about bein' late.

Doug:
Yer always sorry and yer always late!

Antoine:
You boys stop dat naow.
There be plenty time ta cut da trees.
They be here hunnert years,

mus' be they be here at least 'till noon.
Dey ain't gonna raun away.
You boat caum over, warm up, by dis fire,
den we go to werk.

> *The three gather around the fire.*
> *They put their hands out to it.*

> *Doug:*

Where's that log truck? When's he comin'?
We're plugged right up in here. I got no room
to move around. Nowhere to put this stuff.
You call 'im, Antoine?

> *Antoine:*

Yas! Yas!
He say he be here end da week.

> *Donny:*

Either one of you got anything to eat?
I ain't had my breakfast.

> *Doug:*

You're supposed to eat *before* you come!
Listen, boy, this ain't no picnic!
Why didn't ya have your woman for breakfast?
You're the one who's always sayin'
how full a vitamins and minerals
that stuff is. Ought to be you could go all day
on just . . .

Aw, hell! That weren't right. I'm sorry, Donny.
I didn't mean it. It's just that . . .
Ah, never mind.

Doug moves away from the fire toward the crawler

It's just we're earnin' nothin' out here
but our deaths.

*Doug stands in front of the crawler, hands on hips,
and kicks it.
A pause in which Antoine and Donny watch Doug.*

Antoine:
Here's saum coffe an' saum bread
da wimens make last night
an' saum apple jelly.
You still haungry ah got a leg a chicken too.

Donny eats.

How be yer little wimens?

Donny (with a mouthful):
Good!

Antoine:
Good. You babies ever t'ink 'baout maybe yew get married?

Donny:
We're talkin' on it.

Antoine:
Good. Dat be da t'ing ta dew: get married.
Betterin livin' tew yerself.
By Jesus, don't I know.
Ah be 45 before I find my wimens.
Be da best t'ing ah ever dew.

No good ta be alone.
Get married. Haf saumbody be with all da time,
talk tew. Yew werk for each other.
Haf saumbody . . . share.
Get ta be like bein' just one person.

   Donny looks at Antoine and smiles.

   Donny:
Well, I'd better get to work.

   Donny exits toward the woods. Arnie enters.

   Antoine:
Ho! Look who it be!

   Doug:
Christ, hang onto your wallet!
Lock everything up!
Here comes Arnie.

   Antoine:
Wall, Arnie, how you be?
What you up to 'sides no good?
Werkin' naow?

   Arnie:
Naw. Can't find nathin'.

   Doug (who has ambled over to the others
      ostensibly to get some tools):
I bet you ain't lookin' too hard neither.
Can't afford to have a job, old Arnie can't,
always gettin' in the way of his goin' to the jail.
Christ, this county's goin' broke just buyin' grease

to lubercate the jail house door
he's in and out of there so much.

    Arnie (to Antoine, ignoring Doug):
I was wonderin' if you could take me on.
Things is terrible narrow just right now.

    Doug:
Antoine, I'm warnin' you. He comes; I go.
I ain't workin' with him anymore. We'll go broke
just puttin' back all the stuff he steals.
That bastard'll steal the shirt right off your back'
won't ja, Arnie? Why not tell 'im
where you got that jacket.

    Arnie (grinning):
Mountain Company give it to me
when I got done.

    Doug:
Give it to ya, hell.
You stole it and you know it.

    Arnie:
Wall . . . I had it caumin'.

    Doug:
Sure you did. So did we all.
Only maybe you should say how come
you got one big enough for me.

    Arnie:
Only one I could get holt of.

Doug:
Bullshit to that! You're a liar too.
That's the one you stole from me.
I ought to tear that thing right off your back
right now only I couldn't stand to touch it.
It smells too bad.

Doug moves back to the crawler.

Arnie:
Ugly ain't 'ee.

Antoine:
He ain't functionatin' right today.
Got a splinter in his pecker.

Ah wish we had a place fer yew, but just now
we ain't. Da boy down to da woods,
Doug bouncin' 'raound dat crawler
an' ah be here at da landin'.
Nathin' yew could dew. Ah wish dat we could
help yew out. Ah don't know how long we be here
anyway. Dat crawler just about tew caum tew pieces.
Whan dat happen we be done.

Arnie doesn't reply.

How be yer little wimens? I hear da tew a you
be back tagether.

to audience

Yew should see dat wimens.
Meanest beast whatever live.
Uglier 'an a she bear.

Arnie:
Yas, we're back together but it ain't no better.
Just like it used ta be. She's just as ugly
as she always was. Mister, she drinks whiskey
like you used to drink that beer.
I'd be better off livin' with a bobcat.

Antoine:
Wall, dat tew bad. A man shouldn't haf tew wear
'is hard hat in da house.

Arnie:
I know, Christ, if I had money the first thing I'd do
is buy her a funeral. She's good fer nathin'.
Last summer she was sick every mornin'. Get up
puke out her guts. Eats like a pig too. I never seen her
be so fat as she is right now.

Wall, I won't keep ya. Lemme know if you can use
another hand.

Antoine:
Ah will. Ah be sorry, Arnie.

*Arnie exits. Antoine gases up his saw, starts it.
Donny enters from the woods, running, out of breath.*

Donny:
Somebody stole my saw!

Antoine:
What yew say?

Donny:
Somebody stole my saw!
When I got down to where it was

it was gone and there's a fresh pair of tracks
leadin' away toward the swamp.

Doug:
Arnie! It was that friggin' Arnie!
Where's that maul? I'm gonna find that walkin'
piece of kindlin' wood and split 'im down the middle.

Antoine:
Hold on der! How yew know dat it be him?

Doug:
Goddamn you, you soft hearted frog. You . . .

Antoine:
You take yer pecker out yer mouth
put in a turd!
We're goin' lookin' but we're gonna cypher first.

Donny:
Aw, doggoneit, I give two-hundred for that saw.
I'm still payin' on it.

Antoine:
Take it easy. We get it back.

Doug:
That's right and all we got to do
is go right over to Arnie's place to do it.

Antoine:
Now how he steal dat saw?
He be here all dat time, right here wid us,
just a little bita 'go talkin' 'baout a job.

Donny:
Maybe he's workin' with somebody else
and he was up here coverin' for the other guy
keepin' us here while the other guy took it.

   Doug:
Nah, Arnie's too stupid to think a that.

   Antoine:
You don't be so sure. Arnie ain't no dummy.
His head ain't got much shape to it,
but it got some brain inside. I know;
I werk wid him fer years in da Christmas trees.
He ain't as stupid as he looks.

   Donny (to Doug):
Stick up your foot.

   Doug:
Huh?

   Donny:
Stick up your foot!

   Donny looks at the tread on Doug's boot.

You too, Antoine.

   Antoine does the same.

and whose track is that?

   Donny points to the snow.
   Doug and Antoine inspect their boots, make prints, study the other track.

Antoine:
Mus' be Arnie.

Donny:
And that's the track is in the woods.

Doug:
Proof enough for you, Frenchman?

Antoine (quietly):
Yas. Proof enauf fer me.

Donny:
Let's go.

The three begin their exit.

Doug:
Bring a pulp hook, Donny.

By Jesus, mister, when I take holt
that peckerhead an' squeeze
his brain pop out his skull
like a blackhead out a pimple.

Exit all.

ACT II

TIME:
Later that same morning.

PLACE:
Arnie's house, a shack; inside and out.

*In the littered dooryard: junk.
Pieces of cars, a snowmachine,
a dog house, some tractor tires,
an old refrigerator and piles
of rusting, rotting, unidentified rubble.*

*The sagging porch is littered too.
Two garbage cans stand near the door
filled and overflowing with empty beer
and whiskey bottles, a broken couch,
a broken T.V. set, some broken chairs
stacked on top each other, a clothes line
across the porch and the clothes hanging
frozen stiff. And tacked to a post,
a fresh coyote skin.*

*Inside: one room, in a corner,
an old, brown, sheet metal pot burner,
in another, a new, color console, T.V. set,
a couch, some chairs, a chrome and formica
kitchen table, a white, metal kitchen skink,
some metal cupboards, a four burner gas stove,
a double bed, no curtains on the windows
and no shades, a peeling linoleum rug on the floor.
The place is hot and smells like kerosene.*

SCENE:
Gil, Arnie's wife, sits at the kitchen table watching game shows on T.V. and drinking beer.

Arnie approaches carrying a chainsaw. He stops, looks back, then mounts the porch and rattles the locked door.

Arnie:
Open the goddamn door!

Gil:
Who is it?

Arnie:
Open the friggin' door! Hurry up!

Gil (to the audience):
How's a woman 'sposed ta git her chores done
when she's got ta be raunin' back and forth
to the door all the time? A man's work's
from sun to sun, or so the sayin' goes,
only I wouldn't know since the lazy bastard I live with
never worked a day in his life,
but a woman's work is never done.
Who is it?

Arnie:
Hurry up! It's me.

Gil:
Who?

Arnie:
Me!

   Gil:
You?

   Arnie:
Yas, me!

   Gil:
Oh, you. Go away. I gotta watch my shows.
Take a walk in the swamp.

   Arnie:
That's where I been!
Open the door. I got somethin' ta show ya.

   Gil:
Oh no you don't! I ain't openin' my door an'
you ain't showin' me a thing!

   to audience

I ain't never seen anything like it.
He just can't stay away from me.

   she primps herself

Ten o'clock in the mornin' and that's all he can think about.
Never seen anything like it.
Well, he ain't gettin' any.
I got my shows ta watch
and this afternoon I got ta watch the stories.

   Arnie:
Open up, you ugly bitch.
Quit pickin' at those dirty toenails and chewin' on 'em
in your mouth and open the goddamn door!

Gil (to audience):
See how he talks to me? Ugliest man
whatever walked. Got no appreciation.
Who is it cleans and cooks and sews?
Who washes his pants and mends his clothes?
Who cuts up his deer
and buys him his beer?
Who bakes him his bread
and gets in his bed?
He was damn near dead
before I came back
and this is the thanks I get.

Ugly! Why, I ought ta leave him now, again.
I'd do it too if it weren't he needs me so.
Got no appreciation.

Arnie:
If you don't open this door . . .

Gil:
Hold on to that smelly ass of yours!
I'm caumin!

Gil opens the door

Where did you get *that!*

Arnie (smirking):
I got it. An' I can get a hunnert for it too
over to Waterville.

Gil:
You stupid fool! You must like it there
down to the jail. What's the matter

they cook betterin' me?
Well, I ain't bailin' you out again.
I told you so the last time.
You end up there once more,
yer on yer own.

 Arnie:
They ain't gonna get me.
They don't know.
I fooled 'em good. Besides
by the time they figure it all out
I'll have it sold.

 Gil:
Well you had better.

  Arnie gets a beer out of the refrigerator.
  Gil moves to the window and looks out.

Who's this now?

 Arnie:
Huh?

  He looks out the window.

Oh shit! It's them.

 Gil:
Fooled 'em good, you say.
Now what you gonna do?
By the looks of 'em
this ain't no ordinary visit.

   Arnie:
Lock the door!
What we gonna do!

   Gil:
What ya mean, we?

   Arnie:
Yer in this too. They'll bloody *both* our heads.
Think a somethin' quick!

   They both pace, panicked, bewildered.

   Gil:
Go get that little blanket over there
and wrap the saw up in it.
I'll get into the bed and put the saw in with me.
We'll say I had a baby just this mornin'.
They won't believe it
but they'll be afraid ta look.

   Arnie:
Good.

   Gil:
You sit down there, sing a lullabye
and try your hand at actin' natural.

   Arnie does as he is told.
   The pulp cutters approach and hear Arnie
   singing a lullabye mercilessly out of tune.

Antoine:
Mus' be we're too late.
Ah t'ink Arnie killed hisself.
Ah can hear 'im dyin'.

Doug:
Cut the jokes. This here's for blood.

Doug bangs on the door.

Open this door you son-of-a-bitch!

Gil moans
Arnie moves to the door, opens it,
puts his finger to his lips.

Arnie:
Shhhhhhhh . . . she ain't too good.

points toward the bed

She's feelin' awful poorly.
She had a baby boy this mornin'
while I was out
and I be the father.
Weren't just fat after all.

Doug:
Better think a somethin' betterin' 'at, you little twerp.
You know why we're here.

Arnie:
I do?

Antoine:
Seemzo Donny here got his saw stolt,

Arnie:
Naw!

Antoine:
an' we t'ink the thief be you.

Arnie:
Come on, now, Antoine, you know me,
would I do a thing like that?

Doug:
You bet your ass you would!

Arnie:
You hurt my feelin's Doug, but have a look around.
You ain't gonna find nathin'. And keep your voices down
I'm wicked upset at how she is. I'd rather die
'an see her hurt that way.

Gil moans.

Gil:
Who is it, Dear? Who are those men?

Arnie:
Don't pay no mind ta her; she's outin her head
in pain. She just had it, just a little bit ago.
She ain't even cut the cord.

Donny:
Sure she ain't, because a saw won't start
without it.

*The pulp cutters search the house
but stay clear of the bed.*

Arnie:
You boys want a beer?
How about some food.
Got a nice new doe down cellar,
fry you up a steak.

Donny:
We don't want nuthin' but my saw!

Arnie:
What's the matter? Ain't are stuff
good enough fer you?

*Antoine finds a bottle of whiskey in the cupboard.
He sets it on the sink.*

Gil (moaning again):
Honey, can't you make them leave? I've got
ta get some sleep. I'm all wor' dout.

Arnie:
You boys ought to be ashamed!
Your hearts should break.
We don't need this now.
I swear that we be tellin' you the truth
and here's my deal I give as proof;
if we be lyin' I'll go out
and *sell* this child,
my first born son.

Gil moans.

Come on now, why don't ja go?

Antoine:
I can't find a t'ing.

Doug:
Me neither.

Donny:
Doggoneit, I give two hundred for that saw.

Doug:
Comeon, Donny, we may as well go back an' start trackin' in the swamp.

Doug and Donny exit.

Antoine (to Arnie):
Wall, we be terrible sorry t'ink yew be da one. Ah apologize fer allahus.

as he exits

Ah hope you feelin' better, Gil. Ah know yew be; just get saum sleep. An' ah be awful glad tew hear 'bout dat little baby. Congradulations tew yew bot'.

Doug:
Comeon, Antoine!

> Antoine exits. Arnie locks the door. Gil hops out of bed.
> Gil and Arnie laugh; they are delighted with themselves.
> Arnie struts.

Doug:
Goddamnit, I just know that saw is there!
That whole thing was just a lie.

Antoine:
Wall, maybe so, but maybe not.
Yew boys give dat baby anyt'ing?

Doug:
You kiddin' me? The only thing I'd give 'im be
a knock onto his old man's head an' dump him out
behind the barn.

Donny:
Doggoneit,
I give two hundred for that saw.

Antoine:
You boys wait here. I want ta give dat baby somethin'.

> Antoine returns to the house and knocks on the door.

Arnie:
Oh Christ! They're back.

> Arnie and Gil stumble about the room, bumping into
>   each other.
> Gil grabs the saw and hops back into bed.
> Arnie goes to the door, opens it and shouts:

Go away!

Antoine (stepping in):
Don't get me wrong. The odders ain't be here.
I just caum back ta give da baby saumthin'.
All I got's a quarter but at least it's saumthin'.
Ah sure would like ta see dat littl' skipper.

Arnie:
No! . . . You can't.
Don't look! He's . . .
deformed!

Antoine:
Well, dat's alright.

Arnie:
He didn't come out right!

Antoine:
Ah, don't mind.

Arnie:
He's all skund up!
Don't look. Oh please don't look!
It's awful. It'll make you sick.

Antoine moves quietly toward the bed.

Antoine:
Ah jus' wan' a leetle look, eh?

He pulls the covers back.

Antoine:
Ow! He got a long snout!

Antoine picks up the saw and cradles it in his arms as if it were a baby.

Wall, maybe he be hugly but he be yers an' now yew got ta love 'im.

Antoine moves toward the door.

Hey boys! Caum over, see da baby!

Doug and Donny enter.

How you like da littl' t'ing?

Doug:
You bastard! I'm gonna put this pulp hook up your ass!

Donny:
Not if I do it first!

Doug and Donny wrestle with each other for the pulp hook.
Ad lib dialogue.

Antoine:
Now yew boys stop dat talk in front da baby. Quiet down. Can't yew see he's sleepin'?

Donny:
Yeah, and look how rugged he already is; tougher'an a piece a steel.

Doug:
That's no surprise, probably Arnie's already got 'im doin' chores. Yeah, he's ruggid alright,

and that's the only difference, otherwise
he looks just like his father.

   Antoine:
Yas, he do, and ah never see a baby be so young
haf so many teeth!

   Antoine uncradles the saw, carries it now naturally:
Wall, we got tew go tew werk.
We see you later, Poppa.

   Doug:
Hold on there, Antoine.
We got work right here.

   Antoine:
Yew boys can't dew that.
You mighten hurt yer hands
den we all be outta werk.

Nah, we got are saw and that's enauf,
only maybe we just take this whiskey bottle here
and call it resteetution.
What yew t'ink 'bout dat, Poppa?

   The pulp cutters pass the bottle among themselves.
   Arnie doesn't answer. Gil motions to protest but doesn't.

Wall, we caum back soon
haf another visit wi' da baby.

   The three exit with the saw and bottle.
   Lights down on the shack. They walk and drink,
     but only Doug and Antoine drink, Donny refuses the
       bottle.

*Suddenly, there is a young woman, the angel, a waitress,
standing in the road in front of them, her hands
   outstretched
and up, palms turned in — the gesture of a blessing.*

   Angel:
The Lord be with you,

   Doug and Antoine (automatically):
and with thy spirit.

*The pulp cutters have been walking single file,
Antoine in the lead, and when he stops, surprised to see
   her,
the other two crash into him.*

   Angel:
Behold! Be not afraid.
I have good news for you.

And so it was that while they were there
the days were accomplished that she should be delivered.
And she brought forth her first born son
and wrapped him in a dirty old blanket
and laid him on a dirty old bed
inside a broken down shack
because that is where they lived.

And nearby there were pulp cutters
walking down the road and drinking
and the angel of the Lord came to them
and the glory of the Lord shown 'round about them
and they was sore afraid.

Then the angel of the Lord said to them:
I bring you good news of great joy

which shall be to *all* people,
for unto you is born this day a Saviour
who is Christ the Lord.
And he will say to you:

"The spirit of the Lord is upon me,
because He has anointed me to preach good news to the poor.
He has sent me to proclaim release to the captives
and recovering of sight to the blind
and to set at liberty all those who are oppressed."

And here is a sign for you. You will find the babe
wrapped in a blanket, lying on a bed,
beneath that star.

Joy to the world!
Glory to God in the highest!
Peace, good will to everybody!

Go now and be with him.

> *The Angel exits abruptly.*
> *Antoine and Doug look to the star and begin to move*
>   *toward it.*
> *When they are some distance away they realize*
> *Donny is not with them, that he is where he was,*
>   *standing,*
> *head down, dejected. They return to him.*

> *Antoine:*

Yew ain't caumin' wid us?

> *Donny shakes his head "no."*

> *Doug:*

Comeon, kid, come with us.

Donny shakes his head "no," then says:
Donny:
You know where that star is. It's shinin' down on Arnie's house.

Doug:
I guess it is.

Donny:
I ain't goin'.

Doug (quietly):
Donny, we're goin' to see the *baby*.
He can't help who he got for a father.
If people judged you by your folks, you'd be shit-out-of-luck, now wouldn't ya?

Donny looks up.

Comeon, kid, come with us. You know you want to.

Donny (shaking his head):
I can't go with you. I don't believe it.
Things just don't happen this way.

Doug moves to Donny, puts his arm around the boy and hugs him.

Doug:
Maybe not. But let's go see. Let's just go see.
We got nuthin' to lose, Donny, nuthin'.

Then cheerily, trying to pull himself up:

Antoine! open up that bottle. We got to get this boy here
feelin' good. And I'll have another go-round too.
Let's have another drink; then we'll get some presents
and go over there and have a visit.

Antoine:
Yas, Donny, here.
Slug it good.

*Donny takes a long drink.
The other two watch.
Donny coughs, cringes.*

Donny:
But what about our work?

Doug:
Oh, Donny, stuff the work.
You don't like it anyway.
Comeon!

*Doug pulls on him by the neck and the three start off
toward the car.*

Stuffit.
Stuff the goddamn crawler!
Stuff the goddamn saw!

(pause)

Stick a peevee up your ass
and pray for an early thaw!

Donny (warmly)
That ain't bad, Doug. Ain't bad.

The three wander toward an exit.
They have the saw and bottle with them.
As they walk they drink and visit,
and their inebriation, and their joy,
increases.

Donny:
Man, you see that pair of thirty-eights?

Doug:
She wan't wearin' pistols, was she?
I didn't see no pistols, you Antoine?

Antoine:
Naow! But dat don't make no difference to our Donny-boy.
Ah bet he still haffin' versions 'baout
how he got one in each hand.

Donny:
Jeeze, you two are loonies!
You know, if I stay workin' with the both of you,
I'll get like that. I'm gonna get like you.
I will! I got to find another job.

Antoine:
Bah! you stay wid us. We all be rich, maybe tomorrow.
An' if we don't, dan we be lucky 'cause
we still haf' are reason why
we godda get are asses outta bed.

Doug:
Stuff the goddamn crawler
Stuff the goddamn saw.

Donny:
I don't deserve this. I'm too young.

Antoine:
Ain't nobody what deserve anyt'ing.
If you be rich, you don't deserve it.
If you be poor, you don't deserve dat neider.
Pass on da bottle.

Doug:
Stick a peevee up yer ass
an' pray for an early thaw.

Antoine (to the melody of the carol, "We Three Kings of Orient Are . . ."):
We t'ree kings ada puckerbrush are
cuttin' pulp, ea-tin' caviar.
Is it today, or is it tomorrow?
Where da hell iss dat star?

Donny:
I'm too young for this. I'm too young.

Exit all.
The star shines down on Gill and Arnie's shack,
flooding the interior with light.
Mary is in bed with Jesus.
Joseph stands to one side and to the other,
the attending angel.

*The pulp cutters reappear on stage.
Now in addition to the saw and bottle, they have presents
for the baby. Antoine has a toy chain saw; Doug,
a leg of lamb and a sheep skin; Donny has a baseball
   glove,
a catcher's mitt.*

*The three move down stage center and
to the melody of "We Three Kings of Orient Are . . ."
they sing to the audience:*

   All three, together:
We are woodchucks through and through.
We draw pulp, unemployment too.
We get drunk and we get dirty
and we also chew.
   Oh, we got nauthin', never had.
   People think we're worthless, sad,
   but, by Jesus, the angel pleased us
   and we know we ain't all bad.
We three kings of Judevine are,
bearing gifts we brought from the car.
Swamp and back road, with our sack load,
following that there star.
   Oh, we got nauthin', never had,
   but ya know we ain't too bad.
   We are brothers, got each other,
   and the babe, the new-born lad.

   Antoine steps forward.

   Antoine:
Dis here chain saw iss awful small,
but den again da baby ain't tall.

Whan he get bigger, dis be da rig fer
him mak da tree to fall.

Doug steps forward.

Doug:
A leg of lamb, a sheep skin rug,
these are the presents what come from Doug.
One's for the parents, one's for the baby,
and I may throw in a hug.

Donny steps forward.

Donny:
I will give this catcher's mitt.
I love this glove; it's a perfect fit.
Many a game we've played well together;
now to the babe I give it.

All three, together:
Glorious now behold him arise,
King and God and Sacrifice;
Alleluia, Alleluia!
Sounds through the trees and skies.
    Oh, we got nauthin', never had;
    but we ain't uselss, we ain't sad;
    oh, by Jesus, the angel pleased us,
    and we know we ain't too bad.

*The three begin moving toward the shack and the star.
As they do, they sing, to the last two lines of the chorus,
the tempo greatly retarded:*

Alleluia, Alleluia!
We ain't useless; we ain't sad.
Alleluia, Alleluia!
Jesus Christ, we ain't too bad.
Alleluia, Alleluia!
Let's go see the new-born lad.

> *They approach the shack; the angel greets them at the door.*

> *Now the three are little boys,*
> *shy, awkward, delighted.*

> *They push and prod each other to go first.*
> *Finally Antoine puts the real saw on the sink,*
> *then steps forward toward the bed.*

> *Antoine:*

Wall, this ain't be much. Got it down to
the discount store, but maybe it be saumt'in'
dat he like. Be just like da one his Poppa got.
See, yew pull da cord and it go rum-rumrum.
Ah hope da littl' skipper like it.

> *Antoine leaves the toy saw on the bed and backs away.*

> *Donny does not want to approach the baby.*
> *Antoine pushes him forward gently.*
> *Donny can barely speak.*

> *Donny:*

This ain't much of a present either,
but, Jesus, I had some fun with it.
It's a catcher's mitt, ya see?
It's yours now.
You hunker down behind the plate, like this.

>*Donny demonstrates*

And you say, Chuckachucka. Pitchadamitt.
Comeon, baby, Pitchadamitt.
Chuckachucka. Pitchadamitt.

>*Antoine pretends to pitch. Donny throws the ball back,
pounds the glove and says again.*

Chuckachucka. Pitchadamitt.
Comeon, baby, Pitchadamitt.

>*Then abruptly, Donny stands up, embarrassed.*

Well, I hope you have some fun.

>*Donny leaves the mitt on the bed and backs away.
Doug approaches.*

>*Doug:*
My wife and I boochered a lamb last night.
We figured you could use this leg, and this here skin
would make a nice rug for the baby.

>*Doug places the leg of lamb and the skin on the bed
and begins to back away. He pauses, looks down
at the child and says:*

Oh! sweet babe, be careful what you do.
This world is tough; it just ain't built
for all the love you got.
I fear for you. Aw, Jesus Christ!
a man like you was shot.

>*Tableau Vivant.*

>*Blackout.*

Afterword

Pulp Cutters' Nativity is a contemporary adaptation of *The Second Shepherds' Play*, an English miracle play written about 1450 by someone known only as "the Wakefield Master." The play is one of a cycle of thirty-two miracle plays created as didactic theatre to teach the illiterate peasantry the literature of the Bible. Most miracle plays are devout and often humorous dramatizations of Bible stories; *The Second Shepherds' Play* is that and more. The whole play except for a short scene at the very end is an outrageous and warm-hearted parody of the nativity in which a sheep thief, his ugly, cantankerous wife and a stolen lamb comprise the unholy family.

The original play opens with the first shepherd issuing a monologue which is a bitter complaint about the weather, politics and the rich. The second shepherd follows with his own monologue regarding the foulness of the weather and marriage. The third shepherd, a boy, enters and complains again about the weather and asks for something to eat.

Presently Mak, a sheep thief, appears. It is clear that the shepherds know Mak and his penchant for theft. Mak complains that he is starving and that his wife, who is a drunk, is the ugliest, meanest woman alive. He wishes out loud that he could buy her a funeral. Thus Mak passes the time with the shepherds trying to assuage their suspicions. Then, while the shepherds sleep Mak steals a lamb and escapes home to his cottage.

Upon his arrival Mak discovers that the door is locked and Gil, his wife, does not want to let him in. She tells him to go for a walk in a swamp. Finally, after some nasty banter, she opens the door and upon spying the lamb launches into a lecture on how Mak is going to get himself hanged for his perpetual thieving. Shortly however she drops her sermonizing and the two of them begin plotting how they will hide and keep the lamb. Gil suggests she get in bed, put the lamb in the cradle and pretend she has just had a baby. This they do.

Meanwhile the shepherds have discovered they have been robbed. They immediately suspect Mak and head for his cottage. As the shepherds approach they hear Mak singing a lullaby mercilessly out of tune, and Gil, in bed, moaning from the pain of childbirth. The shepherds burst in and accuse Mak of the theft. Mak is insulted that they should think so ill of him. He scolds the shepherds for their insensitivity to his wife's pain telling them their hearts should break with sympathy for the poor woman. Gil swears that they do not have the lamb and as proof of her truthfulness she vows to eat her newborn child if she is proven a liar! Mak then offers the shepherds something to eat, but the shepherds are having none of his hospitality. They search the cottage, staying clear of the wife and child, and find nothing. They are deceived, or at least appear to be, and they leave.

Discovering that no one left a present for the babe, one of the shepherds returns to the cottage to give the child a sixpence and in doing so discovers the truth. The other two return and a scene ensues in which the shepherds hold the lamb and joke about how ugly the baby is and how much it looks like its parents. Mak feebly protests that the baby was bewitched and therefore is deformed.

The shepherds decide they will not beat Mak but instead they take him outside and toss him in a canvas as punishment, a mild retribution indeed in a time when theft was normally punished by death. The shepherds return to the fields with the lamb and fall asleep.

Suddenly an angel appears and announces the birth of Jesus Christ. The shepherds are dumbfounded. They rise and head for Bethlehem following the star which is an interesting and perhaps deliberate confusion since in the gospels the shepherds do not follow the star; the wise men do.

The shepherds arrive at the stable, adore the Christ child and give him three presents: "a bob of cherries," a bird, and "a ball to play Thee withall at the tennis." Then they exit singing and the play is done.

The Second Shepherd' Play was in all likelihood produced on a pageant, a wagon, that moved from place to place in medieval Wakefield. Some scholars suggest that on the wagon for this play there were three scenes: the pasture, Mak and Gil's cottage, and the stable in Bethlehem. They also suggest that two additional actors played Mary and Joseph. These suggestions seem to me, first, uneconomical theatrically and, second, contrary to the author's intention. If there were only two scenes on the pageant, omitting the stable in Bethlehem, then Mak and Gil's cottage could become the stable and if Mak and Gil doubled as Mary and Joseph they could become the holy family. If the play were played in this manner, and it seems to me it could have been, then the implication would be obvious: Jesus was born among drunkards and thieves. That notion is attractive to me; it strikes to the heart of the Christian gospel.

It is clear from *The Second Shepherds' Play* that the Wakefield Master had a well developed political and social conscience; he understood the nature of his society's injustices. He knew the poor man's condition, and he was not afraid to let his characters speak of it acrimoniously. But in addition to his sharp tongue, the writer also had a bubbling and irrepressible sense of humor. Although the play is parody, it is neither sarcastic nor bitter; it is lighthearted, joyful and extremely funny. The Wakefield Master was a good natured fellow and it was impossible for him to speak critically without at the same time seeing the warmth and humor inherent in the situation.

My play follows the original play very closely, almost speech for speech, and within those speeches there is great similarity in content; in fact, in a number of places, where it worked, I used direct translations of the original lines. I have, however, tampered with the original in a few places. The flute player/mime who opens my play is not in the original but I think she is in keeping with the spirit of medieval theatre and with the spirit of this play. I altered slightly the personalities of some of the characters. I gave the angel the nativity narrative as she has it in the original, then added Jesus' first public speech, the declaration of the jubilee year, because I think it is the penultimate message of the gospel. I've moved the singing forward a bit and written new lyrics. I changed the mood of the end. My version ends with a fear, a foreboding for the future; this is the modern age. I made up my own jokes, added a second, more positive, view of marriage and changed time, place, characters and dialect.

I hope my play is not creation or invention, but translation, or better yet, recreation, that is, something old given new life, and something which is an amusement, a pastime, something refreshing, reviving, fun.

What amazed me as I wrote this play was how easily and simply the original transferred from 15th Century England to 20th Century New England, which must be, I am afraid, a commentary on the changelessness of the human condition.

Finally, the central message of the Christian gospel is, in my opinion, that Christ came to give people new life, and new life begins with love for the self. This gift was given originally, and must remain a special gift, to the poor, because to be poor, economically, physically, psychologically, spiritually, perhaps especially in America, is to be told over and over again, every time you turn around, that you are less than others, that you are somehow wanting, that you should be ashamed.

The message of the Christian gospel is a denial of all that; it is an affirmation of self-respect and that is something the poor have never, nor will they ever, get from the societies of Caesar.

David Budbill
Wolcott, Vermont
Advent 1980